L.C.LEWIS

Heavy Haulage

by Paul Heaton

P.M. Heaton Publishing
Abergavenny, Gwent
Great Britain
1996

Front Cover: Volvo FH16 6x4 tractor unit, L16 LCL coupled to a Goldhofer trailer in straight frame configuration and laden with a 50 ton – 60 ft long vessel which was conveyed from the Dow Corning Chemical Works at Barry to Terry Smith and Sons, Cardiff Docks, for breaking up.

Title Page: The Volvo tractor unit, L16 LCL, again coupled to the Goldhofer trailer, but in 2 bed 4 configuration and loaded with 38RB crawler crane with elevated cab, which was moved internally in Newport Docks for W.E. Dowds Ltd.

Back Cover: Foden 6x4 tractor, F132 ATH coupled to an LB45 Tasker trailer laden with a Terex R35B Dump Truck, shown in the Newport Depot of Short Bros. (Plant) Ltd.
and Foden 6x4 tractor unit, E321 SWN conveying a shunting locomotive from British Steel's Panteg Works to the Blaenavon Railway Preservation Society's premises near Big Pit, Blaenavon.

Dedicated by Lewyn and Frances Lewis
to their Parents.

ISBN 1 872006 13 2
© First Edition October, 1996
L.C. Lewis and P.M. Heaton

Published by P.M. Heaton Publishing
Abergavenny, Gwent, NP7 9UH

Printed in Great Britain by
The Amadeus Press Ltd.,
Huddersfield, West Yorkshire, HD2 1YJ

Typesetting by Highlight Type Bureau Ltd.,
Bradford, West Yorkshire, BD8 7BY

PREFACE

Following sixteen years employment in a local factory, as a plant operator and as a lorry driver, in April 1979 with the support of his wife and family, Lewyn Cyril Lewis entered the road transport industry as an owner driver with the purchase of a second hand Gardner-engined Atkinson tractor unit with which he provided traction to other operators. Subsequently and mainly with the help of Short Bros. (Plant) Ltd he became involved in low-loader work, and has built up his business, now operating a small modern fleet of Volvo and Foden tractor units with a wealth of trailers for use on heavy haulage, normally up to 80 tons capacity.

In this book I have set out to cover all aspects of Lew Lewis' career, including his involvement as a plant operator, lorry driver, and through his seventeen years as a haulage contractor. Fortunately many of the individual jobs undertaken by him have been recorded on camera, and I am particularly grateful to Messrs Lyn Thomas, Dario Passaro, Ian Perham, David Stokes, John Shaw, W. Wallace and Lew Lewis for providing the photographs for this book. Additional thanks go to Lew for his patient help with the captions.

Paul Heaton
Abergavenny
October 1996

Young Lewyn Lewis in his pedal car with parents and brother William. (Sister Lynn was born a few years later).

L.C.L EWIS

Lewyn Cyril Lewis was born on March 3, 1948 at the Lamb Inn at Pwlldu, near Blaenavon, Monmouthshire. He attended Pwlldu Infants School which was one of the smallest in the county with less than a dozen pupils, followed by education at St. Peters Junior School and Park Street Secondary Modern, both in Blaenavon.

Pwlldu was a small village situated on top of the mountain between Blaenavon and Abergavenny. It consisted of two rows of houses one of which also served as the village shop, one public house – the Lamb Inn, which is now named the Lamb & Fox and owned by Lew's cousin Brian Lewis, a small farm, and the village hall which doubled as the infants school. Sadly the pub, farm and hall (now an adventure centre) is all that remains.

During the 1940s and 1950s, the mountain above the village was an open cast coal site operated by Taylor Woodrow. The mountain still bears the scars as it was never reinstated. His father Cyril (better known as Nipper) worked on this site as did other members of the family. Subsequently his father worked at the Terpentwys open cast site near the British, Talywaun for Wilson Lovatt driving the walking dragline "Maid Marrion", with his Uncle Will driving the sister machine "Clinchfield". When Lew was aged nine his father took him to work with him on one summer's afternoon, and he recalls that this was the start of his immense interest in earth moving machines. Thereafter, as a child, he would walk miles to watch machines or vehicles working.

The Walking Drag-Line Maid Marrion at Terpentwys Open Cast Site. Cyril 'Nipper' Lewis, Lew's father operated this machine.

Parked on the family's small holding was an old Bedford tipper owned by his father's brother Bert, who had been a petrol tanker driver during the war, and had been driving tippers for various operators, but had been unable to obtain his own carriers licence, it being the days of the A, B and C licences. In this lorry Lew would spend hours driving to all parts of the country. As the vehicle was up on blocks, he had full steering. He would mimic the school bus driver Mr Will (Wrecker) Jones, who drove the local children to school at Blaenavon in his Bedford O.B. coach. He would copy his gear changes using the double de-clutching technique . The slight pause before selecting the next gear up, the blip on the throttle between gears, changing down to bring the lower gear up to the speed of the gear he was changing out of – all to achieve a clean gear change. This much practised technique was to prove very useful in later years during his truck driving career.

When Lew was eleven years old work started on building Llanwern steelworks, and involved the carriage of millions of tons of shale and hardcore to the site. Hundreds of tipper lorries were employed on the project working day and night. His father's cousin Dennis Lewis, who was at that time Plant Manager for Wilson Lovatt at Terpentwys (and later founded the firm of Tecweld Ltd.), had a Thames Trader tipper working round the clock six days a week on this job. The night driver was Wyndham Powell of Govilon, who was often accompanied by Lew's elder brother Bill, who although under age at the time spent many nights driving the lorry. The day driver was Bryn McLoy. Lew helped with the servicing of the lorry on weekends and in refuelling it each day after school. On one occasion the gearbox developed a fault, was taken out and repaired and then replaced no fewer than four times, before it was discovered that Dennis had been looking in the wrong place for reverse gear. On another occasion Bryn was changing a wheel and had the axle jacked up too high and was struggling to lift the wheel on. Lew suggested that he let the jack down a bit so that he would not have to lift the wheel up so high. Bryn – sweating, swearing and in a furious temper threw a spanner at him and told him in no uncertain terms where to go. Lew disappeared in great haste, but peering around the shed saw Bryn letting the jack down and the wheel go on without difficulty.

At fifteen Lew left school and found employment at Pichford and Holland, Blaenavon, manufacturers of furnace bricks. His first year was spent in the metal clad shop where the metal cases for the bricks were made – he hated this work and was forever in trouble with the foreman. By now Terpentwys open cast site had closed and his father went to work at Pichford and Holland in the packing bay stacking very hot bricks from the furnace cars onto pallets to be wrapped and banded ready for despatch by road and rail. Lew was transferred to this department so that his father could keep him under control, and was to be his last chance to keep his job. Fortunately he enjoyed this work and got on well with the new foreman. He spent most of his time driving the fork lift truck, helping his father to stack the bricks or assisting Mr. Harry Harding to wrap, band and pack the pallets of bricks. His favourite job was loading the lorries – which came from all over the country – but the two main contractors locally were Penry Morgan Transport of Blaenavon and S.W. Bowkett of Newport.

A few weeks after his seventeenth birthday he passed his driving test. Unknown to him his parents had saved up enough money to buy his first car. He had had plenty of practice, not only driving the family's Landrover on their small holding, but since fifteen he and his close friend Paul Spence would drive an old car around a small field and over the surrounding mountainside. Only able to afford to buy one gallon of petrol at a time, when they ran out they had to walk the 5 miles round trip to Blaenavon to buy another gallon.

Having his own transport completely broadened his social life, and soon after he met Frances, who by the time he became eighteen became his wife. They settled in Newport, Frances' home town, and Lew found employment as a van driver with the White Rose Laundry, where his young wife also worked. This was followed with a van driving job with Newport Corporation Parks Department and as a labourer with William Adams. Thereafter he was employed as a road roller driver with Naylors Plant Hire of Hereford on hire to Gwent County Council – this gave him the chance he had longed for. When widening the road at Trelleck, a Bristol Plant Hire JCB would dig the verge out, it was then filled with stone and he would roll it. He learnt to drive the JCB and before long had moved on to Cardiff Plant Hire as a JCB driver. At the back of this firm's yard at Caerphilly Road, Cardiff was a large hole used as an inert land fill site, and it was here that he learnt to drive the full range of Cardiff Plant's equipment. From there he worked for many of the major earth moving companies on sites throughout South Wales.

Following six months working for Bryn Motors, Lew became a low loader driver for Jay Dee Transport. His first vehicle with them was an 'A' series ERF 4x2 tractor unit YWD 569J.

Having had an interest in trucks, and feeling the need for a new challenge, in 1974 he decided to obtain his HGV Driver's Licence. He and Frances managed to scrape together the £500 needed for the weeks training course, which he duly passed. The problem with a young man with a new HGV licence, was that very few firms wanted to employ him until he had obtained some experience. However, he managed to find employment with Bryn Motors of Blackwood who were working out of Cwmbran. For the next six months he did a daily trip to Sheffield, carrying 18 ton ingots from GKN, Cwmbran. The tractor unit he drove was a 4 x 2 ERF with a Gardner 180 Engine and six-speed David Brown gear box.

He then had the chance to drive for Jay Dee Transport, a heavy haulage contractor based at Newport. His experience on earth moving machines proved invaluable on this job as he could load and unload the machines himself. This made up for his lack of truck driving experience. The vehicle he was allocated was again an 'A' series ERF, which naturally was the oldest in the fleet. However he was so proud of this old lorry that he would go into work on Sundays without pay to paint her up. Lew states that heavy haulage is the sort of job that you either love or hate, but the loads are so varied it is probably one of the most interesting in the road transport industry. But the hours could be long and wet weather make the job really miserable. On one occasion Jay Dee was contracted to move a Komatsu 40 ton tracscavator which had been on demonstration from Steetly Quarry at Taffs Well near Cardiff to an opencast coal site at Kenfig Hill near Bridgend. Jay Dee's heaviest outfit had been delayed up country, but the move had to be done, and as Lew's vehicle was the only one available he was assigned to do it. Accompanied by his boss, Jim Daw they duly loaded the 40 ton machine onto the four in line trailer, and set off. Having reached the steep hill immediately to the West of Culver House Cross on the A48 Cardiff to Bridgend road, the vehicle broke down – the propshaft having twisted. A brand new 4 x 2 Scammell Crusader belonging to Llewellyn of Wales was brought in to complete the move, and afterwards its fifth wheel coupling was found to be broken in half, such was the weight of the load imposed on the fifth wheel. This ERF ended its working life in Alpha Steel works at Newport, as did the old four in line trailer, on internal work.

His replacement vehicle was an ex-tanker AEC tractor unit. He found it impossible to get a clean gear change, and by the end of his first week with this tractor was ready to hand in his notice. However he suddenly found the correct technique and off he went with a clean change. He drove two of these vehicles for Jay Dee, but found the AEC V8 engine, although very powerful, was very unreliable. One of the last loads he did with the AEC proved to be quite eventful. He was transporting a Caterpillar D8 bulldozer with blade from Newport to Blaina in the North of Gwent, under Police escort with two Gwent motor cyclists. All went well until they reached the Nantyderry junction on the A4042 road, a motorist turned left onto the main road without looking to his nearside and collided with the Police motor cyclist who was riding the centre line signalling to drivers to pull in. Fortunately the officer – P.C. Mike Gunter was uninjured, and he carried on towards Abergavenny with the single Police escort, but at the bottom of the Black Rock Hill, the officer waved a car driver over, the lorry behind pulled in, but the truck behind failed to pull up in time and a collision occurred. The last Policeman had to stop to sort this out, whilst Lew carried on up Black Rock unescorted, with instructions to wait at the top, near Brynmawr. Pulling over to the side of the road, and pressing the clutch to stop, the engine began to rev uncontrollably. He pulled the engine stop, but it did not cut out, unable to get back into gear to stall the engine, he and his mate decided to vacate the cab. The problem with the vehicle was that the engine used to breathe badly and the fitter had piped the breather pipe to the air intake. The engine had got very hot climbing the Black Rock and was running on the oil fumes unrestricted, and he thought it was going to blow up. However, by the time the escort arrived the engine had stopped, and cooled down sufficiently to carry on. Nearing their destination at Blaina, a pedestrian walked round a corner and was struck by the blade which was overhanging the pavement. Fortunately he was more shaken than injured, and finally they arrived at their destination.

The last outfit he drove for Jay Dee Transport was a Scammell Crusader 4 x 2 fitted with a Rolls Royce 220 engine and Fuller Road Range gearbox, this was coupled to a Tasker low loader trailer with fixed ends. Neither the Swan neck nor the rear bogie could be removed. While this arrangement was fine for excavators, wheeled machines were more difficult to load. This trailer later passed into the ownership of M. Stark Plant Hire of Cwmbran, and then to Mogul Plant Hire also of Cwmbran, who converted it to three axles with a beavertail and ramps at the back. It is still being operated, now owned by Hazell's Haulage of Nash Road, Newport, on internal work at British Steel's Llanwern works.

By the middle of 1978 Jay Dee was concentrating more on running steel to the Midlands than on low loader work, and Lew Lewis found this to be too mundane, having to queue to load and unload. He found driving to Birmingham every day that it gave him plenty of time for thought. He therefore decided it was time to take up another challenge. He enrolled at Nash Technical College for a course to obtain his Certificate of Professional Competence (CPC). The course started in September, 1978 and lasted for six months with two classes a week from 6pm to 9pm. Still working for Jay Dee, he found it particularly hard going, as his working day often finished as late as 9pm. He missed numerous classes, but managed to keep up with the work. Only his wife Frances knew of his efforts, so when he passed it came as a complete surprise to his family and friends.

At the age of 31, in April 1979 he took the opportunity to work for himself. Armed with this CPC he applied for and was granted an Operator's Licence – Llewellyn of Wales, hauliers from Newport, offered him traction work if he could obtain his own tractor unit. After discussing it with his wife, he duly made an appointment to see the Bank manager, where with only £66 in their account he persuaded them to lend him £1,500. He went to Neil Platt of Abergavenny Commercials who supplied him with his first lorry – a Mark 1 Atkinson tractor unit with six months MOT for £1,100 plus 8% VAT. Llewellyn's had agreed to supply the fuel, oil and spare parts at cost, plus a service charge. He invoiced them weekly and was paid 30 days from their receipt of invoice. The £312 left from the loan and the £66 in the Bank had to keep Frances, their two daughters and himself for five weeks until the first cheque arrived. Even when he got his first payment it amounted to little more than wages when the deductions for fuel etc had been made. Having an overdraft facility it was important to accumulate as much money in the Bank as possible in case he had a major breakdown. The Atkinson was old and needed a lot of looking after, and Lew found himself working on it day and night to keep it running, not only that but he wanted it to be in first class condition. During the first few months he had renewed everything from king pins and bushes on the front axle to the shakle pins and bushes on the front and rear springs, including the track rod ends. Lew carried out this work himself. This proved to be a considerable drain on his resources, and the family lived on the very bare essentials. It was to be over two years before they considered buying new clothes, and any social life had gone. With Frances's support and encouragement they survived.

When he needed special tools he was able to borrow them from Short Bros. (Plant) Ltd of Cardiff Road, Newport. He had known Mr. Ieaun Short from his time with Jay Dee and they became firm friends. Short's foreman fitter was an old friend of Lew's father Mr Gethin Davies from Blaenavon. Short Bros. had an old four in line trailer in their Newport yard, and when their own low loaders were unavailable, most being based at their Taffs Well yard, and they needed a machine moved, they would call on Lew. As time went by they called upon him more and more, and he found that his old Atkinson, with its Gardner 180 engine and six speed David Brown gearbox, really struggled coupled to the four in line trailer. In October 1979 he part exchanged the Atkinson with Llewellyn of Wales for a Scammel Crusader fitted with a Rolls Royce 220 engine and Fuller 10 speed Road Range gearbox. He liked the Scammell, having driven one for Jay Dee. Shortly after the Atkinson was stolen from Llewellyn's premises at Lee Way, Newport, and was never seen again.

Having operated as a haulage contractor for twelve months, mainly providing traction for Llewellyn of Wales, in March 1980 Lewyn Lewis took the opportunity of acquiring a modern Ford Transcontinental 4x2 tractor unit XDW 1T, seen here in original white and green livery before lettering.

In 1980 a former employee of Llewellyns Mr. Jeff Neal, working for Newport Ford truck sales, gave him the chance to buy a Ford Transcontinental 4 x 2 tractor unit, index number XDW 1T that was being part exchanged by Usk Vale Meats. This vehicle had a Cummins 275hp engine with a nine speed Fuller box, and subsequently he had it uprated by Cummins at Cardiff to 335hp. He made a deal with Llewellyns whereby they took the Scammell back and he obtained from them a 40ft tilt trailer. The Ford was an excellent vehicle which had been new in October 1979 and had only done 5,000km. Lew by now was working for both Shorts and Llewellyns at about fifty/fifty. This suited him well as there was no 10% deduction made by Shorts. Lew also had a Radio Phone installed in the cab for Shorts to be able to contact him at all times.

In March, 1980 he purchased his first new low loader trailer, a Tasker LB 45. This trailer had a six wheel swan neck, and it looked strange to see the gap between the rear of the tractor and the trailer, but he knew that he would need a 6 x 4 tractor before too long, and didn't intend having to change the trailer. Sure enough in 1982 he purchased a six-wheeled Ford Transcontinental tractor unit with a special types plate of 80 tons which was fitted with a 375hp engine, and a Fuller 13 speed gearbox, which had a top speed of 85mph. This vehicle was one of only four right hand drive models in this country of this type. It had entered service with Ford Contractors Plant Division in May 1979, and had been used to take plant on demonstration throughout the country. The vehicle had a blue and white livery, so rather than change, Lew adopted these colours and resprayed the 4 x 2 tractor accordingly. At the same time he named the lorries 'Nipper' and 'Alice' respectively, after his parents.

In 1982 Lew Lewis acquired a modern 6x4 Ford Transcontinental tractor unit, GVX 492T which was particularly suitable for his increasing involvement with low loader work. He is shown here with both his vehicles, resplendent in their blue and white livery.

The latter part of 1980 was very difficult. The recession had slowed work down, so that all he was doing in a week amounted to two full days employment for his vehicles. At this time the opportunity was taken to dispose of the tilt trailer which passed to K.W. Jones Transport of Newport. Lew was all for selling up, but as Frances put it – "We started with nothing, we have nothing, so we have nothing to lose". So the business carried on.

With the arrival of the Ford 6 x 4 tractor (GVX 492T) Lew had intended to sell the 4 x 2 Ford XDW 1T, but it had been suggested by a friend, Mr Kelvin Ward, that he employ John Shaw from Cardiff to drive it. As a result he used the tractor to supply traction for Nessbert Transport of Cardiff.

He was employed by Lew for nearly nine years and proved himself to be a very able low loader driver. Lew worked for Nessbert for twelve months and found them to be a very good firm. By now the low loader work had started to pick up again, and as Short Bros. had not replaced their low loaders as they came to the end of their working lives and as L.C. Lewis was by now based in their Newport yard, he was able to give them the service they required. Short's contracts with the National Coal Board and British Steel meant they had machines working day and night fifty-two weeks of the year. Principally stationed at Shorts Newport depot was the large fleet of loading shovels. As a result on many a night, weekend even on a Christmas day he was called on to change over an unserviceable machine. By this time he had acquired an ex-ARC folding neck Trailmaster trailer and a King TL35 from Shorts. Both XDW 1T and GVX 492T were now employed on low loader work full time.

In 1984 Short Bros. put their big outfit, a 75 ton Foden tractor and 60 ton King trailer off the road. Lew purchased the tractor, but the trailer was not to his liking. Instead he bought a new Tasker trailer, one of the last made by them at Andover, before they became victims of the recession. This trailer was 9ft 6ins wide and extended to 11ft 6ins wide with the out riggers, which made it ideal for the crawler cranes owned by Shorts. He set about refurbishing the old Foden which was a machine really built for the job, she had a Cummins 250hp turbo charged engine, which he uprated to 335hp, a twelve speed Foden gearbox and manually selected reduction hubs on the rear axles, with three position towing jaws back and front. It had a nine ton front axle and two sixteen and a half ton rear axles. Although the Foden only had a 75 ton train weight it was capable of carrying so much more, as he proved on a number of occasions. Fitted with day cab when bought, he fitted it with a sleeping pod, which could be removed or installed as required in just a few minutes. This vehicle was duly named 'Iron Lady Frances' by the drivers. Frances was by now working in the office at the rear of Short's Newport yard, and not being one to mince her words, they had recognised this. With a Specials Types tax of £130 per year, he was able to afford to leave this vehicle in the yard when waiting for work. At this time L.C. Lewis was also respraying machines for Short Bros., the work being mostly on Terex R35 dump trucks and 38 RB crawler cranes

In 1984 he purchased a 75 ton Foden tractor unit, ODW 781R from Short Bros. (Plant) Ltd – one of his major customers.

Expansion of the business continued and eventually the ex-Shorts Foden ODW 781R was replaced by a 100 ton Scammell S26 tractor, index number D940 LKG which was named 'Nipper' (2) (XDW 1T having already been disposed of). ODW 781R is still working at British Steel's Port Talbot works internally for I.C.S. Ltd. The Scammell proved to be somewhat unreliable and was sold back to Leyland the following year at the original purchase price.

He was then offered a Foden test vehicle. This truck was originally a 6 x 4 rigid vehicle with two 16.5 ton drive axles and a 9 ton front axle with a Cummins 400bhp engine, and a 13 speed Fuller gearbox, she had been built by Foden to test its 30 ton rubber suspension. Lew bought this vehicle, had it fitted with a Jake brake and Fairwood Diesel Engineers Ltd. of Swansea converted it into a double sleeper cabbed 150 ton tractor, which he named 'King Billy'. Another Foden was bought new in 1988, this was a 6 x 4 80 tonnes tractor unit with 12.5 ton drive axles and a 7.5 ton front axle, a Caterpillar 400bhp engine with a 13 speed Fuller gearbox. This tractor carried the name 'Iron Lady'

When the Ford 6 x 4 tractor, GVX 492T was taken off the road in 1990 it was replaced by a Scammell badged Leyland Roadtrain twin steer tractor H966 NAX named 'My Lady Alice'. A standard tractor unit with a 320 engine and nine speed gearbox and 55000kg GTW. The decision to buy the twin steer was made because it was to pull the Andover step framed trailer. He also wanted to access any savings in tyre wear and fuel consumption as the double drive tractors were fairly heavy on both counts, especially the rear axle tyres of the double drive tractors.

This 150 tonnes four-axled Leyland Daf tractor, H251 NTX was bought new in 1991.

In 1991 he purchased a four axled Leyland Daf 150 tonnes tractor unit H251 NTX which was named 'Prince William'. This was one of very few of this type in the country at the time and the only one in South Wales. Its 370bhp engine was uprated to 400 by Leyland Daf. This vehicle had positive twin steering, the second axle made by Ginaff carried the same load rating as the two drive axles – 16.5 tonnes each, the front being rated 9 tonnes. The tractor unit could be loaded up to 58.5 tonnes gross, the gear box incorporated a torque converter and retarder, and a radiator stood behind the cab on the nearside to cool the gearbox oil. The second axle and the drive axles had hydraulic suspension. The second axle could have the weight reduced on it to aid traction, and could also be raised when running empty. This vehicle eventually passed to the ownership of Curtis Heavy Haulage of South Humberside, the reason being that the chassis was so long it would not couple to A&T stepframes or ordinary 6x4 necks on other trailers and Lew could not utilise this tractor often enough for his satisfaction.

This tractor was replaced by a Volvo FH16 6x4 150 tonnes unit with a 520bhp engine and C trim cab which gives air conditioning. Lew specified high diffs to maximise fuel consumption and the gross train weight was reduced to 120 tonnes as a result. For his operation the gross vehicle weight of the tractor is most important and with two 16.5 and one 9 tonnes axles the FH16 gives the maximum. The registration number was personalised for this vehicle L16 LCL and the name 'Black Magic' was adopted. One of the main reasons for buying this vehicle was that it can be coupled to the Andover step frame trailers and work under Construction and Use Special Types General Orders categories 1, 2 and 3, and is very suited to the Goldhofer two bed four trailer. In this latter combination it gives a payload of 80 tonnes or more. It was also the first FH16 520 with 'T' ride 2 suspension in this country.

In January, 1994 he purchased a Volvo FL10 320 bhp engined 6x4 tractor built to land fill specification in order to deliver for his customer Terry Adams Ltd ejection trailers full of compressed refuse to land fill sites. This vehicle has a 'B' ride suspension and can work in C & U Cat. 1 & 2 at 55 tonnes gross train weight. L.C. Lewis's latest outfit is a new Volvo FH12 with 'A' ride suspension fitted with a 420 bhp engine and rear lift axle, designed for operation at 80 tonnes gross train weight, and is normally used coupled to a new Andover 41 tonnes gross extendable trailer.

Having operated from Short Bros yard at Newport for many years, the opportunity was taken to acquire premises situated at New Inn, Pontypool, which is ideally positioned to give maximum service to his many customers.

The current fleet operated by L.C. Lewis is:–
F132 ATH - Foden, L16 LCL -Volvo, L230 DAX - Volvo, L12 LCL - Volvo, and retained for yard shunting duties when required GVX 492T - Ford. A host of trailers are in use from an extendable flat bed, through Andover and Tasker low loader and step frames to the Goldhofer 2 bed 4 combination. Note. The Reg No. L10 LCL has been acquired for L230 DAX.

L.C. Lewis is well situated to serve his customers' many needs and requirements with his small but modern fleet of heavy haulage vehicles. He has achieved much in his seventeen years in the haulage industry, and greatly appreciates the customer loyalty he has been fortunate enough to enjoy. He believes that providing the right service is all important in such a competitive industry.

In 1994 this Volvo FH16 150 tonnes tractor unit, L16 LCL entered the L.C. Lewis fleet.

L.C.LEWIS

L.C.LEWIS
PLANT OPERATOR

A48 EASTERN AVENUE, CARDIFF

Lewyn Lewis was employed as a Plant Operator on a number of projects mostly in and around South Wales. Construction of Cardiff's Eastern Avenue is illustrated on this page.

A caterpillar D8 Bulldozer is shown push-loading a Terex TS14 Motor Scraper.

An O&K RH25 Hydraulic Face Shovel at work.

The Face Shovel loading an AEC Dump Truck.

An Aveling Barford 4 Wheel Grader with back and front steering, laying the sub-base of the carriageway prior to the laying of the tarmac.

Lew's cousin Brian loading top soil to cover the verges and banks, using a Caterpillar 950 Loading Shovel.

A Caterpillar D8H Bulldozer with its nearside track off.

BIG PIT, BLAENAVON

Lewyn Lewis was particularly pleased to be involved with the reclamation of the coal tip at Big Pit Colliery, Blaenavon, being so near to his birthplace. Although now closed, the colliery is preserved and is open to the public.

Another view of the Bulldozer minus its track.

Ralph James of Newport driving a D8H-68A Power Shift Bulldozer, without its cab, on the tip.

A D8H-68A Dozer fitted with a cab, but without its blade, is shown pulling Scraper Box.

A Komatsu Crawler Tractor drawing a Scraper Box owned by Short Bros. (Plant) Ltd. The Komatsu was operated by Owner/Driver Alan Webb of Llanelli Hill.

Lew Lewis stood beside his Caterpillar 631 Motor Scraper.

A449 USK TO COLDRA (NEWPORT) DUAL CARRIAGEWAY

Lewyn Lewis worked on the construction of the A449 road. This was the last part of the improvement in the road network linking South Wales with the North.

Caterpillar D8 Tractor and Scraper Box was building up the bank of the River Usk near Kemys when the bank slid down towards the river. The Bulldozer was stuck precariously.

A D8 with blade and ripper was brought up to tow it out.

The steel hawser is connected up. Thereafter the dozer was recovered.

A Caterpillar 631 Motor Scraper is shown bogged down in the mud on the 'haul' road.

Denis Fields pushing a large rock to the site tip with a Caterpillar D8H Bulldozer with ripper.

Another view of Denis Fields' machine.

A loaded D8 and Box on its way to the 'unsuitable soil tip'.

On the 'unsuitable soil tip' Len House is shown driving a Caterpillar D6 Bulldozer in the foreground.

Don Kier of Monmouth trimming the banks of the dual carriageway (the batter) with a Caterpillar D6 Bulldozer.

A Caterpillar 955 Tracscavator loading small rocks onto a Dump Truck for transporting to the site tip.

THE ALBION TIP, NEAR PONTYPRIDD

On this page the illustrations relate to the reclamation of a burning tip.

A Terex R50 Dump Truck.

Royston Wilmer standing by his Caterpillar D9 which was fitted with a cushion blade for pushing.

A D9 Bulldozer push loading a Terex TS24 Motor Scraper.

A 275 Michigan Wheeled Loading Shovel loading a Terex R50 Dump Truck.

The foreman, the famous 'Gypsy' Smith talking to the driver of a 275 Michigan Loading Shovel.

Lew's cousin Brian Lewis driving a D6 Bulldozer landscaping around the source of the Afon Llwyd.

Lewyn Lewis worked on the reclamation of the molton slag tip left over from the old furnaces in Blaenavon.

A Caterpillar D9 Bulldozer push loading a Cat. 637 Motor Scraper.

Another view of a D9 push loading a Cat. 637.

The foreman Tommy Williams from Ebbw Vale with the Bedford Service unit.

A Caterpillar D9G Bulldozer fitted with a sprung loaded pushing blade for push loading scrapers.

Having obtained his HGV Driver's Licence he worked for Bryn Motors of Blackwood for six months. Thereafter in 1975 he became a low loader driver with Jay Dee Transport of Newport. His first outfit with them was this 'A' series ERF with Cummins 220 engine and 6 speed David Brown gearbox. The ERF, YWD 569J is shown broken down on the A48 Cardiff to Bridgend road. She had been conveying a 40 ton Komatsu D155S Tracked Loading Shovel from Steetley Quarry, Taffs Well to the Open Cast Site at Pyle.

Lewyn Lewis also drove this Scammell Crusader 4 x 2 tractor EVH 38L for Jay Dee. She is shown *(above)* outside Stark's Farm, Malthouse Lane, Llantarnam, loaded with a Caterpillar 955 Loading Shovel, and *(below)* at Jones' West Monmouth Grammar School, Blaendare Road, Pontymoile, loaded with a Poclain Excavator which was being transported to Bulwark, Chepstow, for Haywards Plant.

This DAF 2800 6x4 150 ton tractor unit, LHB 247P was loaded with an NCK Ajax C60 Crawler Crane, weighing 65 tons. The outfit is shown: *(opposite)* At the Newport yard of Short Bros. (Plant) Ltd.

(Above) Leaving Short's yard at Maesglas, Newport, turning in the direction of Cardiff, driven by Jim Daw with Ray Fry as Mate.

L.C.L^{EWIS}

Above: Jim Daw was driving this Volvo F88 6x4 tractor unit PDW 194M, which was carrying a 54RB Crawler Crane from Abersychan to Terpentwys. The power steering pump on the tractor had failed, and the vehicle is shown at Victoria Village parked awaiting repairs.

Opposite top: The Daf LHB 247P is shown at Alpha Steel, Corporation Road, Newport, being loaded with a 61RB Crawler Crane owned by Short Bros. (Plant) Ltd.

Opposite centre: The loaded outfit, with the tracks removed from the crane is ready to depart.

Opposite bottom: Shown on arrival at Brighton where the crane was used in the construction of the Brighton Marina.

L.C.L_{EWIS}

L.C.LEWIS HEAVY HAULAGE

Lewyn Lewis entered the haulage industry in 1979 with a second hand Atkinson 4x2 tractor unit with which he provided traction for Llewellyn of Wales. In 1980 he acquired a modern Ford Transcontinental 4x2 tractor unit XDW 1T. This vehicle is shown:

left: Working for Llewellyn of Wales drawing their 40ft box van trailer, waiting to unload paper tubes at Slough.

below: Connected to his own 40ft tilt trailer, parked in a lay by near his parents home at Govilon.

XDW 1T is shown connected to Short Bros.' four in line low loader trailer about to set out for the Phurnacite Plant at Aberdare with a Caterpillar D8H Bulldozer.

The Ford 4x2 tractor is shown on this page connected to Short Bros. Crane Fruehauf step frame tri-axle Beavertail trailer, and is

above: at Short's Taffs Well premises about to set off for the British Steel Corporation Llanwern works.

below: at Aberdare with a four wheel excavator.

XDW 1T in original green and white livery, and still with unlettered cab, connected to his new Tasker LB45 low loader trailer.

above: loaded with a Nordverge Dump Truck. This was the first load carried on the trailer, and the previous night Lewyn's wife and daughter had stayed up late painting it.

below: About to set out from Chesterfield for Llanwern with a new Kockums 30 ton Dump Truck owned by Short Bros. (Plant) Ltd.

The Ford tractor is shown enroute from the Mansfield yard of Short Bros (Plant) Ltd to Port Talbot Steelworks with a Caterpillar 988A Loading Shovel.

Above: Loaded with a Terex R35 Dump Truck XDW 1T is ready to set out from Short's Taffs Well yard for Newport.

Below: Again at Short Bros. Taffs Well premises, this Kockum Dump Truck was destined for BSC., Llanwern. Pictured is Lew's friend 'Taffy' Dave Rogers who acted as mate on this job. Tragically he was subsequently killed in a motor cycle accident.

Lewyn Lewis's Ford 4x2 tractor unit XDW 1T now with lettered cab.
above: Carrying a Komatsu D155A Dozer for Ryan Mining.
below: Loaded with a Hymac 580C Hydraulic Excavator for Jeff Dymond Construction.

Above: Loading a 56 ton 38RB Crawler Crane at Llanwern Steelworks for an internal move on behalf of Short Bros. (Plant) Ltd.

Below: The loaded 38RB ready to be moved.

Lewyn Lewis bought Short Bros. Crane Fruehauf Beavertail trailer. It is shown here in his colours carrying a Caterpillar Scraper Box.

A 32 ton Back-up Roll is shown being carried from BSC Llanwern to Tecweld, Brynmawr.

Carrying a Transformer.

Waiting at Llandore Steelworks, Llanelli to load a Gantry Crane using a hired 40ft. flat trailer.

Short Bros. (Plant) Ltd used to be major hauliers of tar. In this view XDW 1T is coupled to one of their last tar tanker trailers prior to delivery to its new owner on Anglesey.

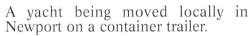

A yacht being moved locally in Newport on a container trailer.

Lew Lewis loading a Terex TS14 Motor Scraper on the Tasker LB45 low loader trailer at Llanwern Steelworks for delivery to Short's yard at Maesglas, Newport. The mate Alan Hemmings is shown.

Above: This 22RB Crawler Crane with 40ft. jib was transported from the Newport yard of Short Bros. (Plant) Ltd to the Usk Flood Prevention Scheme for Welsh Water Authority. The vehicle is seen turning right in Usk onto the Abergavenny road and its final destination. The crane driver is in the cab turning the jib to enable the vehicle to turn the corner.

Below: On the return journey the jib was actually extended to 50ft. and again the driver is seen turning the jib to enable the vehicle to get round the corner.

Above: This Scammell Crusader 6x4 tractor unit, SBO 965Y was borrowed for several months from Llewellyn of Wales in exchange for the Ford 4x2 XDW 1T. The Scammell was particularly suitable for low loader work.

Below: A Ford 6x4 tractor unit GVX 492T was acquired in 1982. She is shown with the 4x2 Ford.

Unfortunately accidents do happen. Lewyn Lewis was driving the Ford 4x2 along the Rogiet to Chepstow Road transporting a road roller when the chains securing it broke, and the roller slid onto the road surface, but fortunately no one was injured. The photographs show:

Opposite top: The road roller is seen where it came to rest on its side on the road surface.

Opposite bottom: The mobile crane arrives and positions itself ready to lift the roller.

Above: The mobile crane rights the roller on the road surface before reloading it onto the trailer.

Below : The road roller is reloaded onto the low loader trailer. Note the all steel deck of the trailer.

L.C.L EWIS

When acquired in 1982 the Ford 6x4 tractor unit GVX 492T had blue and white livery, and it was decided to adopt these colours for both his vehicles. This view shows the two vehicles in the new livery. GVX 492T had originally been used by Ford Contractors Plant Division to carry plant on demonstration throughout the United Kingdom. It was a modern vehicle fitted with a 375hp engine and a Fuller 13 speed gearbox.

It was an extremely useful vehicle for low loader work, and with its 80 ton plate gave a new dimension to the L.C. Lewis fleet.

L.C.L<u>EWIS</u>

The L.C. Lewis fleet in 1982. The group comprises *from the left:* Lewyn Lewis, driver John Shaw, Lew's nephew William Lewis and Alan Tunicliffe who sprayed XDW 1T.

The group standing in front of the two Fords in Short's yard are *from the left:* Phillip Roberts (Short Bros. foreman fitter), nephew William Lewis and Lewyn Lewis.

XDW 1T shown carrying a Fowler steam roller FF 4910 from Barry Docks to Tredegar House, Newport.

Another view of the Fowler steam roller enroute to a steam rally at Tredegar House, Newport.

The Ford 4x2 is shown coupled to the Nooteboom 4 axle step frame trailer having loaded the track frames for a 1405 machine. The driver was Peter Kuck.

With the adoption of black livery for the fleet in 1988, XDW 1T was so painted, but sold before the cab was lettered. She is shown having just loaded the track frames, jury mast and jib section for an NCK 1405 crawler crane belonging to Short Bros., at the Isle of Dogs. The crane base and cab was carried on another L.C. Lewis vehicle.

The 6x4 Ford Transcontinental transporting a 32 ton Back-up roll from Llanwern Steelworks to Tecweld, Brynmawr.

Lewyn Lewis had to recover this Berliet tractor unit following a collision on the A449 Monmouth to Coldra Road. A low loader had to be used because the damaged vehicle's chassis had been severed just behind its cab.

Another view of the recovery of the Berliet lorry on the A449.

GVX 492T drawing the former Short's Beavertail trailer laden with a Scraper box.

A 35 ton Gradoll 1000 Excavator fitted with a hydraulic hammer attachment, being loaded at the Newport yard of Short Bros. (Plant) Ltd.

The Ford Transcontinental GVX 492T was named 'Nipper' after Lew's father. In this view John Shaw has just loaded another Gradoll 1000 excavator, at Shorts.

The Hydraulic hammer attachment can be clearly seen in this view.

In this photograph Lew Lewis is driving the Ford 6x4 laden with a Gradoll excavator, and is leaving the M4 Motorway at Tredegar Park enroute from Llanwern Steelworks to Short Bros. yard at Newport.

A Motor Yacht being loaded at Christchurch, Hampshire for delivery at Swansea Marina.

A 38RB Crawler Crane loaded on a new Tasker LB80 Triaxle low loader trailer drawn by the 6x4 Ford.

Above: John Shaw on the trailer with Paul Ivermee chaining down.

Below: The outfit is ready to leave Short Bros. Taffs Well Depot.

A Finley Highway Mobile Screening Plant which was towed from Short Bros. yard at Newport to the Phurnacite Plant at Aberdare.

A Priestman Lion Crawler Crane which is seen here after being loaded at McAlpine's premises at Crick which was transported to Newport.

A Face Shovel and equipment which was transported from the Open Cast Coal Site at Hirwaun to the North of England.

An NCK Pentland Crawler Crane which was delivered to Barry Docks from Bridgend.

GVX 492T transporting a new Caterpillar 988 40 ton Loading Shovel.

A Ford H50CK Excavator enroute from Manchester to Short Bros., at Newport.

An Oil Pipe Line vehicle being carried on the Tasker LB80 trailer, but using the Swan neck from an LB45.

A new 60 ton Mobile Stone Crushing Plant being delivered to Southampton docks for export from Brown & Lennox at Pontypridd.

A Terex R50 35 ton Dump Truck being transported to Birmingham is shown waiting on the A5 for a Police escort. Driver John Shaw is standing by the cab.

This photograph of the same load gives some idea of the size of the dump truck. Driver's mate Paul Ivermee is pictured.

GVX 492T coupled to an LB80 trailer is carrying the TL30 King Trailer with the Ford 4x2 tractor XDW 1T on top. They were enroute to Liverpool to collect a crane and jib sections.

A Caterpillar D8 Dozer being transported from Short Bros. Barnsley Depot to Taffs Well.

A Caterpillar 988A Loading Shovel carried on the LB45 trailer about to leave Port Talbot Steelworks for Taffs Well

Part of a Coal Washery being conveyed from Blackwood to Scotland for Ryans.

A Komatsu 155 Bulldozer and blade waiting near the 'Little Chef' North of Monmouth for a West Mercia Police Escort.

A Bristol Channel Pilot Cutter which was carried from the South Coast to Bristol Marina where it was restored.

Cwmbran Carnival with Frances *(right)* and daughter Julie.

The first new Andover SFC 36 trailer.

Two views of a Crest Slag Carrier which was brought from Liverpool Docks in parts to Hecketts at Port Talbot where it was reassembled.

Two Carnival Queens —

Above: XDW 1T carrying the Cwmbran Woodland Players.

Below: GVX 492T The Greenmeadow Playgroup's 'Wizard of Oz'.

Above:
The Ford Transcontinental 6x4
tractor unit GVX 492T shown in
black livery in 1989. This vehicle
remains in the L.C. Lewis fleet but is
used solely for yard shunting now.

Left:
Lewyn Lewis was often employed by
Short Bros (Plant) Ltd. to spray plant
and equipment. Shown here is a
Terex R35B Dump Truck at their
Newport yard.

L.C.LEWIS

Two views of Short Bros. Foden 6x4 75 ton tractor unit ODW 781R coupled to King tri-axle trailer. This vehicle was fitted with a 250hp Cummins turbo charged engine and a 12 speed gearbox. The outfit is shown helping L.C. Lewis out by transporting a 60 ton Back-up roll from Llanwern Steelworks to Tecweld, Brynmawr for refurbishment. In 1984 this tractor unit was bought by Lew Lewis and repainted in blue and white livery. He also sent the vehicle back to Cummins to have the engine uprated to 335hp., and named it *Iron Lady* after the affectionate title given to his wife Frances by the drivers.

ODW 781R coupled to the Tasker LB70 tri-axle trailer was transporting an NCK 1405A Crawler Crane from Port Talbot Steelworks to Blaina Wharf, Newport, for Short Bros. (Plant) Ltd. Nearing its destination at Canal Parade the outfit was travelling on an unmade road with deep ruts, when the fully oscillating fifth wheel on the tractor unit allowed the trailer to dip into a deep rut and although the ballast of the crane was well blocked up, the jolt broke the retaining chain and allowed the ballast to swing round. The trailer had to be jacked up and the 78 ton crane re-aligned, before it could complete its journey.

The Foden 6x4 tractor unit, ODW 781R is shown coupled to a 4 axle Nooteboom extendable stepframe 90 ton trailer on fluid suspension (water and anti-freeze) which L.C. Lewis had bought from Richard Marston Ltd., of Pontypool. The outfit driven by Melvyn Watkins is shown transporting a 35 ton steelworks rolling mill spindle from Tecweld, Brynmawr to the British Steel Corporation, Port Talbot works, following reconditioning.

Another view of the Rolling Mill spindle in transit. The wrong number plate is displayed on the trailer.

A 22RB crawler crane minus its jib and a Caterpillar 988 bucket weighing a total of 25 tons being conveyed from Port Talbot to Taffs Well for Short Bros. The Foden is driven by Melvyn Watkins with Paul Ivermee as mate.

60

ODW 781R transporting an NCK Rapier 605-2C Crawler Crane from Ipswich to BSC., Port Talbot on behalf of Short Bros. (Plant) Ltd.

A Priestman Lion Crawler Crane weighing 35 tons being carried from McAlpine's Depot at Crick to the Whitehead's Steelworks at Newport.

A 45 ton NCK Rapier crane being transported without its tracks from Short Bros. premises at Taffs Well to a site in London. The Foden is fitted with it's detachable 'sleeping pod'.

On this page and facing:

A Bell measuring 16ft 6ins wide and Hopper at 19ft 2 ins wide being transported from Port Talbot Steelworks to Tecweld at Brynmawr for renovation.

The tractors used were the Foden 6x4 ODW 781R – Hopper and the Ford 6x4 GVX 492T – Bell.

A Shunting Engine was transported from the site of the old South Celenyn Colliery to a Preservation Society's premises in Yorkshire for Mr. Harry Needle.

Above: Mr. Needle drives the locomotive onto the bed of the Tasker LB80 trailer.

Below: The Foden tractor unit with Swan neck is brought back into position and reconnected to the trailer, then the locomotive is secured in position.

Overleaf: The Foden ODW 781R and trailer slowly make their way across the railway line as they leave the colliery site at the beginning of their long journey.

Left: A 61RB Crawler Crane being loaded onto a tri-axle trailer at W.E. Dowd Ltd., Tredegar Wharf, Newport. This view shows the tracks being removed from the crane before it is transported.

Below: The 61RB leaving Dowd's premises at Church Street, Newport, in charge of the Foden ODW 781R.

Left: On arrival at BSC., Llanwern the Swan neck is disconnected from the trailer.

Right: The tracks are lifted into position and refitted to the crane.

Left: The reassembled Crawler Crane is driven from the bed of the trailer.

Left: An NCK Andes C41B Crawler Crane which was taken from Short Bros (Plant) Ltd., Taffs Well to British Tissues, Maesteg.

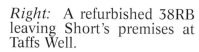

Right: A refurbished 38RB leaving Short's premises at Taffs Well.

Left: A Komatsu 455 Bulldozer (with blade and ripper) weighing 80 tons enroute from Gelli, Rhondda to Measham, West Midlands.

Left: A Coal truck is winched onto a 2 axle King trailer at Coed Ely for delivery to the Welsh Industrial & Maritime Museum, Bute Street, Cardiff, for renovation and preservation.

Right: An 80 ton Stripper Column for the steel industry which was conveyed from BSC., Port Talbot to Tecweld, Brynmawr. This was actually the Foden's maiden trip for L.C. Lewis, before the cab was lettered.

Left: An Aveling & Barford Dump Truck enroute to Jeff's Earthmoving Equipment at Bridgend.

NEWPORT
GWENT

(0633)
213814·57336

The first new tractor unit to enter the Lewyn Lewis fleet was this Scammell S26 100 ton vehicle, D940 LKG. Fitted with a Cummins 350hp engine it had a 9 speed Fuller gearbox with four deep reduction gears.

It became the second vehicle to be named 'Nipper' after his father.

In this photograph the trailer's Swan neck is still connected to the tractor unit and a railway wagon is being winched into position on the trailer bed.

Lew was disappointed with this tractor as it proved to be unreliable in service. No small operator could afford to have a vehicle out of service, and subsequently it was sold back to Leyland.

L.C.LEWIS

D940 LKG transporting a Michigan Loading Shovel.

A Molten Metal Ladle which was transported from BSC. Llanwern to S.H.E. Engineering, Cardiff.

The Scammell 100 ton tractor transporting an NCK Andes Crawler Crane from Short Bros. (Plant) Ltd., Taffs Well.

A 22RB Crawler Crane being carried for Ryan Mining.

Delivering a Caterpillar CAT 235 Excavator for Ryan's Mining from Cardiff to Gelli Washery, in the Rhondda.

D940 LKG at Southampton Docks delivering a 45 ton Henley Fork Lift Truck.

Above: Part of a Washery which was transported from Pontllanfraith to a Ryan's Mining site in Scotland. The Ford 6x4 carried the other.

Below: An NCK 1405 Crawler Crane which was transported from Hecketts at Port Talbot to the Midlands for breaking up for scrap.

An NCK 1405 Crawler Crane about to leave Short Bros. at Taffs Well for London.

D940 LKG and GVX 492T photographed at Tecweld, Brynmawr about to set out for Port Talbot Steelworks with parts of Cut Off Shears as used in the steel industry.

A barge which was used for coal reclamation in a pond at the old Phurnacite plant near Aberdare, being carried on the 4 axle Nooteboom trailer extended. Note the terrible conditions that the Scammell had to go through to deliver her load.

A Terex R35S Dump Truck being carried for Jeffs Earth Moving Plant of Bridgend.

Lewyn Lewis's brand new Foden 6x4 tractor unit, E321 SWN on its maiden job. An NCK Andes C41B Crawler Crane had been left on its trailer parked overnight at J.M. Watkin's Westgate Garage, Llanfoist, Abergavenny, in the shadow of the Blorenge Mountain. The Foden was sent to complete the journey to the Midlands.

Above: The outfit pulls out of J.M. Watkin's yard, and

Below: Turns onto the Llanfoist Slip Road, making it's way to the A465 Heads of the Valleys Road.

In 1987 L.C. Lewis acquired this Foden 6x4 tractor unit, E321 SWN through Fairwood Diesels, Foden's agent in Swansea. Fitted with a 400bhp Cummins engine and a 15 speed Fuller gearbox, the vehicle had a gross vehicle weight of 150 tons. It had been a rigid test vehicle used by Foden to test their 30 ton rear suspension. It was converted at Foden's factory at Sandbach into a tractor unit for Lew, and he had Fairwood Diesels convert the single sleeper cab into a double.

With this new tractor unit he adopted the now famous black livery, and named the vehicle 'King Billy'.

With its arrival the earlier Foden, ODW 781R was taken out of service and sold.

In the photograph E321 SWN is seen conveying a shunting locomotive from the British Steel Corporation's Panteg Works to the Blaenavon Railway Preservation Society's premises near Big Pit, Blaenavon. The driver was John Shaw with Dilwyn Jenkins riding as mate.

L.C.L<u>EWIS</u>

The Foden 6x4 tractor and tri-axle trailer transported a Terex 85 Dump Truck from an Open Cast Coal Site near Glynneath to another site at Castleford in Yorkshire.

Above: The dump truck is reversed onto the bed of the trailer.

Below: The Swan neck is recoupled to the Tasker trailer before the front wheels of the dump truck were removed.

Above and below: The outfit breaks its journey for the night at J.M. Watkin's yard at Llanfoist, near Abergavenny. Pictured is Lew's father Cyril 'Nipper' Lewis.

Above: The hull of a steel yacht is loaded by crane from the garden of a private house, at Llantarnam, and

Below: Conveyed to the Star Trading Estate at Ponthir, near Caerleon.

E321 SWN *(King Billy)* is seen transporting a 45 ton shunting engine from Wales to the North of England.

Another shunting engine is taken from Deep Navigation Colliery near Nelson to the Rhondda Heritage Park at Porth again on the Tasker LB80 trailer.

An Electric Motor for a Walking Drag Line is conveyed from Swansea to an Open Cast Coal Site, at Nantheen, Onllwyn.

Above: Foden 6x4 Tractor E321 SWN and Tasker LB80 trailer carrying a Molton Metal Ladle from Llanwern Steelworks to S.H.E. Heavy Engineering for refurbishment.

Below: Transporting a steam railway crane from Cwm Coke Works to Rhondda Heritage Museum at Porth.

Acquired in 1988 this Foden 6x4 tractor unit, F132 ATH conveyed a steam roller DW 5880 for Mog Thomas from Llantwit Major to a Steam Rally at Tredegar House, Newport.

Lewyn's wife Frances and daughter Sarah join in the fun at the Steam Rally.

This Steam Ploughing Engine *Sandringham* was transported from Marshfield to the Great Dorset Steam Fair on behalf of its owner James Louther.

A 60 ton Mobile Stone Crushing Plant which was taken from Wenvoe Quarry to Thomas's Quarry at Lydney.

F132 ATH coupled to a Tasker LB45 trailer after it's conversion into a tri-axle. The rear axle lifting when required.

[0633]
2139M·57336
NEWPORT
GWENT
L.C

This Foden 6x4 tractor unit F132 ATH was bought new in 1988 and was built to Lewyn Lewis's own specification. Fitted with a 400bhp CAT engine and a 13 speed gearbox, he had specified Kenworth rear suspension. Named *'Iron Lady Frances'* she remains as a unit of the present fleet.

She is seen with a Terex R35B Dump Truck on a LB45 trailer which was being carried from Jeff's Earth Moving Plant, Bridgend to Southampton Docks. Permission was given by Short Bros. to park overnight in the yard at Taffs Well.

L.C.LEWIS

A 40 ton Hitachi 181 Excavator is shown carried on a 3 axle Tasker low loader trailer enroute from Short Bros. Taffs Well yard to Llanwern Steelworks.

The Tasker LB45 trailer is loaded with a 45 ton Back-up Roll being transported from Port Talbot Steelworks to Tecweld, Brynmawr.

A new Submarine Work Platform weighing only 6 tons enroute from John Curran Ltd., Cardiff to Barrow-in-Furness.

A Lightning Fighter Aircraft which was taken from British Aerospace, Preston to the Rhoose Aircraft Museum.

Another view of the Lightning Aircraft, this time being unloaded at Rhoose.

The Foden 6x4 tractor F132 ATH is shown working with an Open Top Refuse Ejection trailer from the Monmouth Borough Council tip at Llanfoist to Terry Adams site at Yanley, near Bristol.

A Steel Vessel i. moved internally a Llanwern Steelwork: on a 41 ton extendable Andover step frame trailer.

An RDO 33 Dump Truck being loaded at a quarry near Aber-y stwyth for transit to Jeff's Earth Moving Plant, Bridgend.

The Foden F132 ATH shown coupled to a refrigerated trailer which his brother William had recently purchased.

This 42 ton Liebherr Excavator was being conveyed from Cardiff Docks to a roadworks site on the A449 Raglan to Coldra (Newport) Road, and is shown in a lay-by at Pentwyn Pitch, Pontypool.

Another view of F132 ATH with the Liebherr 942 Excavator.

The first Andover trailer Lew Lewis ever owned – the 36 ton SF36 stepframe loaded with an ARC Powell Duffryn BK170 Tarmac surfacing machine and two road rollers.

This Catamaran was built in a warehouse at Splott, Cardiff. It was transported by L.C. Lewis to Penarth Marina, placed in the water and sailed to Oban where it was used for training divers. It is shown:

Opposite top: Being lifted by crane into the street at Splott.

Opposite Centre: John Shaw is shown reversing the trailer under the load.

Opposite bottom: The boat comes to rest on the trailer where it is secured.

Top: The boat is lifted from the trailer and about to enter the water at Penarth Marina.

Above: The boat is ready to set out for Oban.

This Scammell 6x2 twin steer tractor unit, H966 NAX was bought new in August, 1990. Fitted with a Rolls Royce 320 Eagle engine it had a 9 speed Fuller gearbox and was named *My Lady Alice* after Lewyn's mother. By agreement delivery was delayed so that it could be used in a 'Truck Pull' by the athlete Geoff Capes at Cardiff Fruit Market.

It is shown:

Top: As delivered coupled to L.C. Lewis's first Andover trailer.

Above: Carrying Nash Rocks paving machine.

Opposite top: Shown carrying a Claas Combine Harvester and cutter from Penhow to Fishguard enroute for export to Ireland.

Opposite bottom: Carrying a Motor Yacht from the Southampton Boat Show to Swansea Marina the outfit pauses at the Leigh Delemare Services on the M4 Motorway in order to fuel the boat with 4 star petrol. All part of the L.C. Lewis service – although goodness knows what the petrol attendant thought.

Part of a Submarine Working Platform is shown leaving the works of John Curran Ltd., Cardiff for Barrow-in-Furness.

This fishing boat *CF46* was conveyed from Splott, Cardiff to Cardiff Docks.

A Pipe Bridge being transported from Rowecord's Newport Depot to Llantrisant in Mid Glamorgan. The Load weighing 20 tons and with a length of 50ft. was carried on an extendable trailer.

Imported through Newport Docks a Furnace Wall for the Rechem Plant at New Inn, Pontypool. This load was 19ft. wide.

A Motor Yacht about to leave the Swansea Yacht Haven for Windsor Marina.

A new kiln comprising of twelve individual loads was transported from Cardiff Docks to Aberthaw Cement Works. Shown is the Scammell 6x2 tractor H966 NAX driven by David Stokes and mated by Andrew Traylor, with the Foden 6x4 F132 ATH driven by John Shaw.

In March, 1991 Lewyn Lewis purchased a four axled Leyland Daf 150 tonnes tractor unit, H251 NTX which was named *Prince William*. This was the first of this type in South Wales. Its 370bhp engine was uprated to 400 by Leyland Daf in this country.

It is shown:

Above: About to depart from the British Steel Corporation's Llanwern Works for the Blaenavon Railway Society at Big Pit, Blaenavon, with a Shunting Locomotive. The Driver was Lewyn Lewis with mate Andrew Traylor.

Below: Waiting for a Police Escort just off the M4 Motorway at Port Talbot whilst enroute from Glasgow to Llanelli with a Terex 3811 Dump Truck weighing 75 tons and measuring 16ft 4ins high by 15ft 10ins wide.

The Leyland Daf 8x4 tractor had been built in Holland by the manufacturer's 'specialist heavy haulage tractor division', and arrived in Britain painted white. Lewyn Lewis went with his father Cyril 'Nipper' Lewis to fetch it from the Leyland Daf compound at Colchester. They are pictured, proudly taking delivery.

With Newport Transporter Bridge in the background the Leyland Daf is seen moving a 38RB for W.E. Dowds Ltd from Newport Docks to Tredegar Wharf, Church Street, Newport. Because the journey was only a short distance and there were no bridges on the route the jury mast on the crane was not lowered.

This 45 ton Electrical Rotar was enroute from B.E.R.L., Cardiff to the north of England.

The first Andover trailer with power steering ever constructed was built to the order of McIntosh Plant of Scotland. The manufacturers used L.C. Lewis's Leyland Daf tractor unit to test it. With a 45 ton neck and four 16½ ton axles it provided a payload of 80 tons. It is now owned by Short Bros. (Plant) Ltd.

A 56 ton 38RB Crawler Crane is shown enroute from Short's Newport yard to Swansea Docks on hire for coal handling.

A total of four of these 40 ton Caterpillar articulated Dump Trucks were moved from the site of the Blackwood-Pontllanfraith Bye Pass to Avonmouth docks, for John Jones Excavation.

This impressive view shows the L.C. Lewis Leyland Daf 8x4 tractor unit, H251 NTX coupled to a Tasker tri-axle trailer carrying a Terex 3811 Dump Truck from an Open Cast

Coal Site near Glasgow to another near Llanelli. Lewyn Lewis, driving and mate
Andrew Traylor pause on the A74 Southbound for a Police Escort.

This view of the Leyland Daf shows a Crawler Crane being transported.

A 38RB Crawler Crane is seen leaving Short Bros. Taffs Well Headquarters for their Port Talbot Depot. Note the Leyland Daf's long range fuel tank mounted on the neck of the trailer.

The outfit is shown Northbound on the M5 Motorway near Weston-Super-Mare.

When sold in 1993 the Leyland Daf passed to Curtis Heavy Haulage of Humberside. She is shown in their colours fitted with a ballast box at Truckers transport cafe on the A40 South of Ross-on-Wye.

In January, 1994 this Volvo FL10 6x4 tractor unit, L230 DAX was bought in order to deliver for his customer Terry Adams Ltd ejection trailers full of compressed refuse to land fill sites. Because it came in white and was needed in service immediately it wasn't painted in the L.C. Lewis black livery. It is shown *above* coupled to an Ejection Trailer and *below* with the Goldhofer 2 bed 4 trailer.

The Volvo FL10 is pictured *above* delivering a Caterpillar 215 Excavator to roadworks on the site of the Cwmbran Bye Pass, and *below* with part of a Conveyor System which was transported from Cwmbran to Bournemouth. This vehicle is normally driven by Tim Barry from Abergavenny, and is named *Nipper*.

This Volvo FH16 6x4 150 ton tractor unit, L16 LCL was bought by L.C. Lewis in 1994 and is fitted with a 520bhp engine and Volvo's own 16 speed gearbox. Because it has high diffs fitted it is down rated to 120 tons. A vehicle that Lew Lewis is particularly proud of, he has named it *Black Magic*. It is shown *above* transporting a 38RB Crawler Crane with elevated cab and rigged for grab internally within Newport Docks for W.E. Dowds Ltd. The trailer used is the Goldhofer in 2 bed 4 configuration.

Below: A Euclid R50 Dump Truck weighing 35 tons is carried on a Tasker tri-axle trailer from Jeff's Earth Moving Plant, Bridgend to Southampton Docks for export.

110

Above: A 50 ton vessel transported from Barry to Cardiff Docks on the Goldhofer trailer which was used in straight frame configuration.

Below: A 45 ton NCK Andes C41B Crawler Crane which was carried from a road works site at Port Talbot to Cardiff Docks.

Above: L16 LCL with Goldhofer trailer in low loader configuration laden with 50 tons of counter weights for a mobile crane. Moved from Hewden Stuart Crane Hire Ltd., Cardiff to London.

Below: A former United States Army tank owned by William Davies which was transported from Penarth Road, Cardiff to the Midlands.

Above: A Nicholas Skip Carrier for use in the steel industry which was taken from Lackenby Steelworks, Yorkshire to Port Talbot for Hecketts.

Below: The Volvo 6x4 and Goldhofer trailer with a 45 ton Back-up Roll used for rolling aluminium ingots into coils which was returned to Alcan at Rogerstone from Tecweld, Brynmawr following refurbishment.

A Caterpillar 988B Loading shovel taken from BSC., Port Talbot to Newport Docks for Short Bros. (Plant) Ltd.

The Goldhofer 2 bed 4 trailer showing the forward two axles raised for running empty.

A Short Bros. 38RB Crawler Crane being taken from Allied Birds Fragmentation, Rover Way, Cardiff, to Panteg Ponds, at Panteg Steel Works, near Pontypool.

A Terex 3307 Dump Truck at the Bridgend Depot of Jeff's Earth Moving Equipment on arrival from Buxton, Derbyshire.

A 36 ton Scrap Vessel being moved internally at Tremorfa Steelworks, Rover Way, Cardiff.

This 40 ton Mobile Scrap Baling Plant was taken from Engineering Services Bridgend to Falkirk in Scotland.

Two views of an NCK Orion HC80 Crawler Crane which was transported from the Texaco Oil Refinery at Milford Haven to Newport Docks for Hewden Stuart Crane Hire Ltd. The trailer used was the Goldhofer with the Volvo FH16 drawing. In the upper photograph in the background can be seen the Foden F231 ATH which carried the jib section on an extended platform trailer. Driver David Stokes checks his load.

Above: An Aveling Barford RDO Dump Truck which was taken from Jeff's Earth Moving Equipment to Southampton Docks.

Below: A Fiat Hitachi 220 Excavator which was taken from Blaenavon to Abersychan.

Above: The Volvo FH16 L16 LCL and Goldhofer trailer in two bed four configuration carrying a Mk 2 Challenger tank from near Salisbury to the Castlemartin Range in West Wales. One of thirteen which travelled in convoy.

Below: The same outfit carrying another tank in convoy in the South of England.

Above: A Fowler Steam Roller which was carried from West Wales to a Museum in Cornwall.

Below: A 30 ton excavator undercarriage which was transported to Port Talbot Steelworks.

Quite a small load by the standards of L.C. Lewis. A 22RB Crawler Crane with extra

counter weight is taken from Neath to London by the Volvo L16 LCL and tri-axle trailer.

Above: Seen with the Volvo FH16 is the as yet unlettered Volvo FH12 6x2 tractor unit, L12 LCL, which is fitted with a lifting rear axle. Bought new in 1995 it is fitted with a Volvo 420bhp engine and 16 speed gearbox. Plated for 80 tons G.V.W. she carries the name *Lady in Black.*

Below: Shown in the New Inn yard of L.C. Lewis, the Volvo FH12 is coupled to a tri-axle trailer.

Above: Loaded with a Nash Rocks Paving machine.

Below: Volvo L12 LCL about to return a Refuse Ejection trailer to the New Inn Refuse Transfer Station of Torfaen Borough Council.

Above: A 32 ton Back-up Roll enroute from Llanwern Steelworks to Tecweld, Brynmawr. The outfit has paused in the lay-by on the Blackrock Hill for a short time.

Below: The Goldhofer trailer in 6 axle stepframe configuration is seen carrying a Transformer from the SWALEC Sub-station at Cwmbran to a new Sub-station at the Mamhilad Industrial Park.

Above: The Volvo L12 LCL which is named *Lady in Black* is shown transporting a Kress Carrier from Grimsby Docks to K & J Services at Rhymney, to be refurbished.

Below: JCB JS130 Excavator being moved locally for H.Williams and Son, Goytre, Gwent.

Above: Moving 80ft long piles on Cardiff Docks in connection with the Cardiff Bay Barrage. Because this involved an on site journey the 40/60ft extendable trailer was used.

Below: This tractor unit is driven by Carl Dee, whose father had been the low loader driver for Beavis Plant of Risca.

Above: A 41 ton Back-up Roll being transported from Llanwern to Tecweld, Brynmawr.

Below: The extendable platform trailer loaded with Hewden Stuart Crane Hire's jib section and out rigger mats.

Above: The Volvo tractor L16 LCL and Goldhofer 2 bed 4 trailer carrying a vessel from D.M.D., Ferry Road, Cardiff to the new Japanese Television Glass factory at Ocean Way, Cardiff in March, 1996. Overall length of the outfit was 90ft. By using the trailer's hydraulic suspension the height of the load was reduced to 17ft, and grossing 70 tons.

Below: A Gradol 880 is shown at Llanwern Steelworks.

L.C. Lewis is a Member of the Heavy Transport Association